Tippi
My Book of
Africa

PHOTOGRAPHY **Sylvie Robert and Alain Degré**

Alain DEGRÉ et Sylvie ROBERT
sont heureux de vous faire part
de la naissance de leur fille

TIPPI

Le 4 juin 1990   Windhoek (Namibie).

P.O. Box 5774
Ausspannplatz 9000
WINDHOEK
NAMIBIE

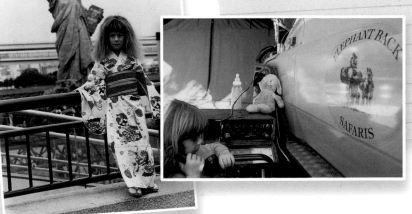

I dedicate this book
to my old companion,
Leon the chameleon.

Tippi

I wanted to write wild sentences

Tippi is my name. I am African, and I was born ten years ago in Namibia. Lots of people ask me if I spell my name like 'teepee' as in 'Indian teepee'. My parents named me after Tippi Hedren, the actress who starred in The Birds, a scary movie by Alfred Hitchcock.

I'm happy my parents named me Tippi for many reasons: first of all, there are not many other girls named Tippi, which is okay with me because there are also not a lot of other girls who have lived like me. This name also reminds us of the Indians who lived in the wild, just like me. And finally, Mr Hitchcock's movie is called *The Birds*, and I love animals enormously. I'm not exaggerating when I say enormously.

The animals are like brothers to me. It's normal. I was born and raised with them. These wild animals of Africa were my first playmates, and that's why I know them so well.

Tippi is my first name but my whole name is Tippi Benjamine Okanti Degré. My last name, Degré, comes from my parents, Alain and Sylvie. They are wildlife photographers who came to live and work in Africa. It's because of their work that I was born in Africa. My first middle name, Benjamine, was given to me to thank Benjamin, a friend of my mom's who gave her accommodation for several weeks when I was born. My parents lived in the bush and giving birth to a baby in the wilds of Africa is not always possible. So when I was ready to be born it was Benjamin who helped my mom in Windhoek, a city in Namibia where there is a hospital.

My other middle name, Okanti, means 'mongoose' in the Ovambos' language. Ovambos are one of the peoples of Namibia. It may seem funny to call your daughter mongoose, even if the word Okanti sounds lovely! It's here where my story begins . . .

Before I was born, my parents spent seven years living and working in the Kalahari Desert. The Kalahari Desert is located in southern Botswana and borders on South Africa and Namibia. For all these years, they observed, photographed and filmed meerkats, which are adorable little mongooses. You won't find meerkats anywhere else in the world.

The meerkats soon became 'family' to my mom and Dadou (that's what I call my Dad). Even though the meerkats are wild, it was they who adopted my parents. I know that this was a really great time for my mom and Dadou, a time without any worries. They were so happy living in the Kalahari Desert with the meerkats, I'm sure they would have liked to spend their entire lives there if they could have. If my mom had had the choice, she would have given birth there, so I would have become a 'little meerkat girl', to be like a sister to the meerkat family. But it never happened.

One day, my parents got into an argument with some men who had different ideas and who didn't believe in my parents' work. And because they were in command, they chased Mom and Dadou out of the Kalahari. Sometimes humans are so stupid . . .

I was born a few months after my mom and Dadou left the Kalahari. I never got to see the world of the meerkats, except in the photographs and films taken by my parents. But I still feel that I am part of the meerkats' family because my name is Tippi Benjamine Okanti and I know how to talk with animals.

Everyone is intrigued when they find out that I can talk with animals.

Everyone but the animals! I am always being asked again and again how I learned to talk to animals. It's boring! I don't have much to say . . . I don't want to explain how I talk to them, because it's useless. It's a secret. You must be gifted to understand. Everyone has a gift whether it's to write, to sing, to paint, to learn other languages, to do sport. All gifts have some kind of mystery.

Understanding animals, this is my gift. Not any kind of animals: only wild animals from Africa. I speak to them with my mind, or through my eyes, my heart or my soul, and I see that they understand and answer me. They move, or they look at me and it seems that letters appear in their eyes. Then – I know it may sound weird – I'm sure I can talk to them. This is how we become acquainted and sometimes we even build a friendship.

Well, that's life. We have all been given gifts and mine is a little bit special. I know it is a great treasure and deep in my heart I hope that I'm the only one to have this gift. Because, like all treasures, we would rather keep them for ourselves.

Tortoises always
look grumpy.

My Nono is nice and soft, he smells good and he is an inseparable friend. Every time I go and live somewhere I leave my friends behind, and it's the same with the animals. We meet, we become friends and then I leave. With my Nono it's not like that; every night he is here with me.

And sometimes my Nono has accidents. One day, a caracal (which is a kind of lynx), cut my Nono's head open. Luckily I wasn't there to see it. I don't know who sewed it all back together. In his life, he has had plenty of holes as well. But we have always been able to fix him. Right now he has a white tummy, but his heart and one of his legs are made out of panther's skin. It looks good!

I have never lost my Nono, but we have forgotten him sometimes, but that's no big deal because all we have to do is make a U-turn and go back and get him – even though it makes my parents furious when we have to go back and drive an extra 100 miles on badly beaten dirt roads, all because of my Nono.

Forgetting my Nono in another country scares me terribly. That is why I have two spares, but it's not the same at all.

I don't know from what age I will no longer need my Nono; perhaps never. For me, I believe I will have him just until the day I meet my boyfriend and fall in love. I also believe it's possible to sleep with your boyfriend and your Nono. It's not because you care so much for your Nono that you're still a baby.

I also have a toy chick. Its name is Angel, because inside is the soul of my baby chicken who died in Madagascar. My Nono doesn't have a soul because I didn't name any dead animal after him. I must say that I have never had a bunny rabbit.

I have already slept without my Nono. At least five times.

Abu is my 'brother'. He is an elephant, yet he is an adult and more than 30 years old. He has a funny story too. Abu is an American elephant! I know it may seem strange, but that's the way it is. I met Abu in Africa, in Botswana, at Randall Moore's place. Randall is a friend of my parents and is completely crazy about elephants. He has taken in plenty of elephants that have come from all over the place. He built a place just for the elephants and it's like a village in the Okavango.

There's a secret that makes it very easy to know the origin of an elephant: if the elephant comes from Africa, its ears are the shape of the African continent and if the elephant comes from Asia, its ears are the shape of India.

Randall feeds, cares for and raises the elephants like family. In exchange, the elephants give visitors rides and they also help in making movies. Among them there is Abu. Randall and Abu used to work together in an American Circus. They became such good friends that when Randall left to go and live in Africa he brought Abu with him on the ship!

Abu is a magnificent character, my friend, my 'brother'. I love him, it's as simple as that. It gives me so much happiness when we are back together. I don't know if there is a better place to sit than behind his head, with my legs stuck in his ears. With elephants this is the only place that is really soft. The rest of their bodies is covered with thick hairs that are really scratchy.

I'm so happy when I'm on top of Abu that I could stay there for hours and hours.

Abu weighs five tons but he never squashes me. That is the way elephants are: they pay close attention to little ones.

Steady, Abu! Get up, Abu! Move on, Abu!
That's a good boy! Abu is an 'English
speaking' elephant.

I know nature. I know the paths. I know where
I am going and I never get lost.

My mom loves this photo a lot. It's in black and white because all of the other cameras that took colour pictures were broken that day. My parents had been staying at the camp but I was with Randall and Abu who were making a movie for Walt Disney. It was really hot and when you're shooting a movie, you wait around for hours and hours doing nothing. I was too little to remember it but I can very well imagine what happened: Abu and I were probably fed up, so we left. Mom told me that she saw us both show up out of nowhere. I had got rid of my nappy and my shoes – apparently I used to do that all the time – and I walked on my tiptoes so the big chunks of dried mud that covered the ground would not hurt me. Mom says that Abu followed me like a baby sitter and she said it seemed as though he was walking on his tiptoes to be careful not to squash me.

Racism, I don't like this. I don't know what could have been going on in the heads of racists. Often it's because of different beliefs that people don't get along. Each person would like everyone to believe in his God. It's stupid. Everyone has a right to believe in any God they want. And racists also dislike differences in colour, language, hair, and customs . . .

Me, I have the blood of an African but I am white. There are lots of people that are white in Africa. The colour of skin should not matter at all. But I don't know how to explain that to the racists. I'm not trying to fix all the problems of the world. I was not put on earth for that reason. If I could save some animals it would be a good start.

Sometimes I have fog in my mouth.

27

The treasures of the Himbas are their goats, cows and bulls. They don't have money.

One day they planned a party for me. They love children. They are so kind. They put some magic powder all over me so that I could become a real Himba.

The magic powder smelled bad. It smelled like goats. It's made with magic rocks that are found in a secret cave.

In life it's a good thing to have nice surprises even if they are really small. All you have to do is not forget to look at what is beautiful.

Someone once told me an African tale explaining why an ostrich has a long neck. It's that way because the ostrich tried to pull its head out of the jaws of a crocodile that was trying to pull it into the water. Because the ostrich was really strong, it pulled in the other direction, trying to get its head out of the crocodile's strong bite and its neck stretched longer and longer. The crocodile became tired, so he finally let go.

It's really fun to be on the back of an ostrich. It's soft and it keeps you warm. It's really comfortable.

I met Linda, an ostrich, who was part of a big herd. The ostrich breeder has a big herd of them and sells their meat and feathers. In southern Africa, they dry the meat with spices that make it taste good. It can become very tough so you have to chew it for a long time, but it's really delicious. It's called biltong and I adore it.

Ostriches are not dangerous but you still have to be careful. On the bottom of their feet they have something like a really pointy fingernail (called an ergot). If a predator attacks them they can cut its stomach open with the ergot and the predator dies because the ostrich has a lot of strength.

Linda was really nice. She was so afraid of making me fall off that she didn't want to move. It's too bad because I would have really loved it if she had run. I love speed! Especially when they run, ostriches are the fastest birds in the world.

It's easy not to confuse a cheetah with a leopard. A cheetah has two big black tears that make him look sad. He's a lot less dangerous than a leopard and you can also tame him.

I met J&B at Dawid and Peta, who lived near Windhoek in Namibia. They bred big herds of cows in the mountains. In that region the farmers have big problems: to prevent the leopards from chasing their cows, they set cage traps for them. That's how Dawid and Peta found J&B. His mummy was caught in a cage and during the course of that night she gave birth to two babies, one male and one female. The farmer found the mother and cubs the next morning. They were separated and placed in game farms and Dawid was given the young male. He named him J&B.

Even though Dawid and Peta gave him the bottle and raised him, J&B was never tamed. He is a leopard and a leopard is dangerous. I knew that but I was never afraid. I played with him and he could feel that I was not afraid of him so he never attacked me. He was so cute. When I saw that he was going to do something naughty, I would scold him really hard and then he would stop and look at me with a look of hurt.

One time, I was playing with him and he took my shoulder in his mouth. He didn't close his jaw, otherwise I wouldn't have my shoulder today but his teeth scratched me a little. I could really feel that he could easily have gobbled me up, if he wanted to . . .

And then there was that horrible time when I went for a walk with Mom, Dadou and Leon, the chameleon. J&B heard us leave and wanted to come with us. He climbed on the roof of the house and then jumped over the top of the garden fence without asking anyone's permission first.

On the way he ran into two little Africans. When they saw J&B they were really, really scared so they started running and screaming. They didn't know that when you are facing a wild animal that is exactly what you must not do. J&B immediately took them for his prey and caught the smallest boy . . .

My parents and I saw it happen without being able to help. Mom said, 'I'll run and get Dawid.'

And she hurried towards the house. Dadou said to me in a stern voice, 'Tippi, you stay here and you don't move!'

He left me there with Leon to save the boy that J&B had caught. I watched Dadou take off running but I couldn't help it, so I finally followed him.

J&B was a few feet from his prey in a position to attack. He had blood in his mouth.

I heard the voice of Dadou speaking to him softly as he took the little boy in his arms. And I could tell that J&B did not want to let this little boy go. I believe that he had really decided to jump on Dadou to get back his prey. Perhaps then he would also have attacked Dadou and that made me really, really mad. Someone had to make J&B stop. I walked up to him and I said, 'J&B, stop it!'

J&B only understands English because that is what you speak in Namibia. And to be sure that he understood me well, I gave him a tap on his nose. It was a hard little tap so that he could understand that he was being a 'bad boy' and that he must obey me or I would be very, very angry.

So he sat down and he gave up, and just like before when I had scolded him, he had a hurt look on his face.

After Dawid arrived, the little boy went to the hospital. Luckily it was a small wound. I will never forget the boy's big terrified eyes as he watched J&B. He was sure J&B was going to get him. And he was right to think that: I really believe J&B could have hurt him.

In my opinion, Dadou too was scared stiff. But he never told me that. He doesn't talk a lot, my father.

J&B was punished a lot. They locked him up in a cage with wire netting all the way up to the ceiling. He could no longer leave, but I went to see him, to speak with him and to pet him through the wire. That made him so happy that once he peed on me to say that he loved me. I didn't want to wash myself because I wanted to keep the smell of his friendship with me, but Mom said it was out of the question. I had to take a shower and she scrubbed me really hard.

This story shows that having a leopard is a very big responsibility. It's a very strong animal and it can kill people. Even so, J&B was cute, and we loved each other very much.

Crocodiles only think about one thing: eating. So to take this picture with a baby crocodile we had to put an elastic band around its mouth. Otherwise it would not have minded taking a bite at me.

Crocs are a little bit disgusting to touch: cold, rough and not at all cuddly.

And for this picture in the water, we didn't even need an elastic band! Dadou and I were playing the game 'danger' with a plastic crocodile, and it was a lot of fun.

The day you meet a child or even an adult who plays with a crocodile, it will be a miracle. In reality crocodiles are very dangerous. Dadou has already had his bottom bitten. Once. And it hurt him a lot.

My Dadou thinks he is old, but it's not true. He has been young for a long time and the lines on his face are just to make him look handsome.

It's difficult to describe Africa. There are billions of differences between Africa and France. Billions.

Often, people say that I am Mowgli's little sister. And I don't mind because Mowgli is wild, and I am wild too. I cannot really explain it. All the little girls I know are domestic, except me. I am wild because I lived in Africa, far from cities, and also because I consider animals to be my family.

I often think I would love to go back. It was an extraordinary life there. I don't know why we always have to leave. Problems begin when we enter towns.

Dadou told me that in Botswana, while driving along, lots of tsetse flies often got in through the windows. They are big flies that sting real hard. Well, they always rushed to sting him, but they never touched me. Dadou still wonders why. I think it's a mystery . . . maybe they felt I was from their world but not my Dadou? Or it might just have been a matter of smell or taste? Not everything can always be explained in life.

Because there are no baobabs in towns, I have to climb street lamps.

Salaams
to Tippi
@ X Xmas 1998
Peter Beard

Peter Beard is a famous international wildlife photographer. He gave me an autograph that I like very much for his wonderful book on elephants called *The End of the Game*. Here's his hand print and a message.

We can be friends with a tree or whatever we like. What counts is the imaginary world. It's part of the imagination to love a tree, because it's beyond reality. Normally, we love people or animals, but not plants. It's possible to love a rose because it is beautiful. Or a tree because it is nice: this is unreal, a nice tree. Animals are nice for real, but a tree, it doesn't move, it doesn't talk, it doesn't watch . . . so how could it be nice, if it does nothing?

I don't think God exists but
he made himself alone.

A zebra is beautiful, but not very interesting. It looks like a horse with stripes, except for riding: you can never climb on it. Zebras can't be trained. It's almost impossible to ride or to tame zebras.

One day in Africa, someone gave me a crystal. I wondered if talking to the sky with this magic stone in my hand would give me some sort of power. So I tried. I went towards a giraffe to see if I had the power. Normally if we try to get close to a wild animal, it runs away. But this time, she came towards me quietly. When Dadou arrived, she ran off. It's a pity, because concerning the magic stone, I will never know.

Whon I was little, I believed that a porcupine had porcuspines!
A porcupine is beautiful, but people who want to touch one are
crazy. If someone fell on one he would be pierced because its
spines prick real hard.

My parents told me that we have never been really good friends with baboons. When I was little and we were living in the bush, in Botswana, the trees were full of baboons. Their favourite game was to pinch my bottle to nibble it. Apparently it used to make me mad!

When I was four I met Cyndie. She was a baby, almost like me. But she was a baboon. At the time, I couldn't tell the difference between a baby baboon and a baby human. For me, Cyndie was a friend, that's all. We used to climb everywhere together, and we even shared my bottle! It was disgusting but because I was little, I didn't mind. Cyndie and I became inseparable.

I went away on a trip for a long time, and one day, I met Cyndie again. I was so happy to see her! She had grown a lot, much more than I had. My parents asked the people where she lived if it was dangerous to play together again. They said that there was no problem.

In my country, in Namibia, it is said
that Bushmen are the only humans
who understand the baboon's language
and that they can even speak to them.
That's because they believe that baboons
were humans a long time ago.

I would like to do
something to protect
nature, but I have
no possibilities.
I should ask God.

No problem! My foot! As soon as she saw me, Cyndie jumped on me to pull my hair. Even if she was only a little baboon she already had a lot of strength. She hurt me a lot and most of all made me feel very sad. I don't know what happened in her head: I was coming to see her again and she immediately attacked me. The grown-ups said she was jealous of my hair. Honestly, I don't see why . . .

I cried a lot and I lost a lot of hair, and since that day, I hated that Cyndie, even though I knew it was not her fault.

Friendships with animals are not like friendships with humans. Animals always have enemies; it's the logic of nature. We must show them that we are the strongest otherwise they will dominate us. Maybe Cyndie wanted to dominate me? But we had spent so much time together that she should have remembered my smell and also that we were the best friends in the world. Apparently animals' memories are not the same as ours . . .

We must not believe that the animals' world is perfect. The truth is that there are many difficulties, and also a lot of violence. For example, meerkats lose their babies most of the time because smart jackals steal them and eat them. Then the meerkats are filled with sadness. Because meerkats have much love.

As for reptiles, I don't know. Chameleons for instance: I know lots, lots. I think they have love but I'm not sure. When males mate with the prettiest female, is it love?

I don't know if chameleons fall in love. I think so but I'm not sure, because I am still little, and I have not lived my life long enough, even if I am ten and entering my adult life.

As for the soul, it's the same: I know that bugs have not got one – we cannot even speak with them – but the other animals? I think they do have one, but first of all I have to believe in God to be sure of that. And even more, I will really only be sure when I am dead.

Why wasn't I created in English? I adore English.

A lion cub is so adorable. This one's name is Mufasa. He was soft, so soft and so funny! We played a lot together. Once we even had a nap together and while we were sleeping he sucked my finger.

When we met one year later, he had grown up. By magic he had become enormous. He recognised me and came up to play with me. He gave me a caress with his tail, but he had so much strength, even in his tail, that it made me fall over!

My parents were not at ease, so they preferred me not to stay with Mufasa. It's a shame, but that's the way it is. When we don't really have trust, it's better not to persist. Actually, it's exactly the same with humans.

I have no room left in my
dreams for nightmares.

When elephants are old, they leave alone to die somewhere. It's said that they leave for the elephants' cemetery, but nobody knows if it really does exist. Maybe they make it anywhere, as long as it's far away from everything. They can't go much further so they die on their way. It must be hard though, to try not to die.

I don't really believe in God. Actually I believe in Him, but I cannot be sure until I have seen Him. I'm not even sure we have souls, and that we can go up to the sky for another life afterwards. Maybe we're some kind of robots and when we die we're in the dark and we no longer exist at all.

Elephants cry salty tears, just like us.

My Dadou told me that an elephant's brain weighs six kilos, and that it's four times the size of ours. That's why they have a big memory and know everything. And in his trunk he has more than fifty thousand muscles. So he has a lot of strength.

When I tell a secret, I find
it hard to say the words,
especially if it's a deep secret.

Wild people always believe in at least one god but I don't know if it is God. I think that their god is an animal. Maybe for them, all the animals together make one god. I don't know . . . what I am sure of, is that I dislike people that believe too much, because they are closed in and we get the impression that they are not free and that God decides for them. I get cross when someone decides for me.

I say prayers, but I do realize that I provoke the voices in my head. I cannot help it; I make them come. And if I don't think about them anymore, there are no voices. I never believed that God spoke to me, but it disappoints me a lot: I'd like to hear a voice that doesn't come from me. Soon, if He really doesn't want to talk to me, I'll end up not believing in Him at all. Also, I have the impression that He doesn't take much care of the planet. Anyway, I can't really see what He does for the moment . . .

That's why I don't really believe in God. I believe much more in guardian angels.

There are humans that are nasty for no reason, just for fun. These people come from the bad. I don't know if this exists in the animals' world. If an animal came from the bad it would never ever be nice to anybody, and there would be no hope in becoming its friend. It must be strange. Me, I have never met one, maybe just crocodiles?

It's the same for snakes. Everybody believes that they are nasty. Me, I have never been bitten by a snake, but by a meerkat, yes. That's why in some pictures, I have teeth marks on my nose. It was not his fault! He was very stressed. When I got near him to take him in my arms, he felt unsure and he bit my nose to defend himself. I couldn't hold it against him.

Animals, I think, always come from the good. Not from the bad.

The future is the present and the present is the past.

83

One day, I met three meerkats at some farmers who had adopted them. Because Mom had been telling me stories about meerkats since I was little, I had the impression I knew them before seeing them. They are really very, very cute.

Sometimes I wonder if my mom doesn't have magical powers to communicate with meerkats. But I don't really want to believe this because it makes me a bit jealous. Maybe she can only speak to them but she cannot understand them? Anyway, she only speaks to them with her mouth. Me, I speak to them through my eyes.

I'm very happy to be called Okanti and to be part of the meerkat's family. It's a wonderful family. They spend their whole life taking care of one another. Alone, they can't do anything, but together they are much stronger than any other animal.

And they are the kings of cuddles. Meerkats' cuddles are very special. My mom taught me how to make them. We hold each other in our arms and we do squeezing hugs.

It's lovely.

'Aren't you afraid? How do you manage not to be afraid?' This is the question that everybody asks me, especially the adults. Of course I'm not scared, otherwise I wouldn't go near them. When I'm with the animals I'm never scared, but I feel impressed sometimes. It's not the same thing at all.

But I must admit that I know animals because I was born amongst them. And my mom and Dadou taught me the dangerous things. For example, a yellow cobra, well, if you touch it you're dead. But a python, if you give it cuddles and you tickle it on the tummy, it won't hurt you. These are things you have to know . . .

I don't know how many times I've heard Mom or Dadou repeating to me, 'Never be scared but always be suspicious.'

Or, 'What must we do when we see a snake?'

I know the answer by heart:

'We don't go near it, and we run fast to go and get Mom or Dadou to ask if it is dangerous. If it is a dangerous one, we're careful not to come face to face with it. And if it's not, we can become friends.'

Actually, it's the same with all animals. Once we understand that, there's no reason to be scared.

Often, the animals are scared of humans. That's why they growl, or they give you a nasty look: to impress you and to make you want to leave them alone. And when they're too frightened, they sometimes pee on you. But not on purpose.

Lots of the animals I have met are used to seeing humans. It doesn't mean that they are tame, but they live in places where humans often come to visit them, like in reserves (really huge parks, where animals are free). And sometimes they even live together: man and animal.

I would never go and play in the way of a wild elephant, or scratch the head of a leopard I don't know! I'm not completely crazy. I don't want to be crushed by a herd of elephants or eaten by a wild cat.

That's to say, even if some of these animals are friends with humans they remain wild above all else.

So you'd better be careful. The thing is to watch out that they never come to think that you're their prey or a danger to them. For example, never turn your back on them or stay on the ground if you fall. You must just look out for them the same way they look out for you.

Of course I say I'm not scared but I must admit that I am from the earth and not from the sea. So, don't count on me to visit piranhas or a great white shark.

Animals are never nasty, but they can be aggressive. I gave up explaining to the whole world that we must not say 'nasty animal' but 'aggressive animal'. It's useless; nobody wants to understand. What can I do? I'm not going to spend my entire life explaining the same things . . .

Animals are aggressive when they want to protect themselves, their young or their territory. And also when they're injured or in a bad mood. Or just because they were born that way. Anyway, they always have a reason. It's not like humans: often, humans don't even know why they are nasty. For instance, sometimes when I'm angry, I'm a real witch. Horrible words come out of my mouth and I don't even want to stop them.

One day I absolutely wanted to meet Elvis, but the adults didn't really want me to. Of course Elvis is a big male baboon, very strong and very impressive. Everybody thought he was aggressive and no one could tell what his reaction would be. I don't know why, but my heart told me I could go towards him. Finally my parents let me.

The adults recommended that I especially not look him in the eyes. He would have taken this as a challenge, as a kind of provocation, which would have made him furious. So I only watched his hand; I approached with mine very, very slowly. It works this way with animals. We must touch to get to know each other. Smell is also important.

Elvis sniffed me; he must have felt that I was not an enemy to him. I gave him a friendly caress. He kept very still. It's funny, a baboon's hand. It's hot and very hairy. It looks like a human's hand.

When I moved away a bit, Mom and Dadou looked relieved. I was happy to have met Elvis. It nearly reconciled me with baboons, even if we did not have enough time to become friends.

In life there is great happiness and many misfortunes. And sometimes things are just normal. When we lived in Namibia, it was especially normal. We only had the usual worries, and sometimes great happiness, but never huge misfortunes. Over there our life was really great.

When I came back to France, I did try to talk to sparrows, dogs, pigeons, cats, cows and horses. But it doesn't work. I don't know why. I think it's because my real country is Africa, not France.

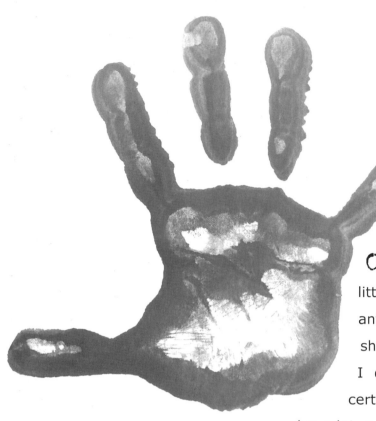

One of my favourite pictures is one of when I was little: we see my hand close to the mouth of an antelope. An antelope is frightened of its own shadow, but this one wasn't even scared of me. I don't remember what happened, but I was certainly talking to her. Otherwise, why would she have let me approach her, me the horrible human, coming from the race that kills the antelopes?

Dadou took the picture, and afterwards the antelope left because she had lost concentration or she forgot to stay calm. In fact, it's difficult to stay calm in front of somebody who scares you.

When I think about it, when I see this picture, I say to myself that it's really weird, this gift that enables me to talk to animals.

Love of animals is something where quarrelling has no place. Or if we quarrel it's different to the way we do it with humans. I don't know why it's so different. But I think it's because animals manage with what they have whereas humans always want something else.

My mom says that Bushmen are the humans who are the closest to animals. They have known how to live in the wild for hundreds and hundreds of years, maybe thousands.

Because they haven't known civilisation, they haven't changed any of their habits. Normally to them, time and money don't count.

I met them in the Kalahari Desert and in northern Namibia. I'm really lucky to have met the Bushmen. They don't often go near white people.

The first thing I would like to say about them is that they are very, very beautiful. Often, they look old but it's because of the sun that burns their skins so hard that it gives them wrinkles, even the youngsters.

They are kind too. They always laugh. Men seem to perform as in a comedy; they imitate animals and play the fool to make the children and women laugh.

As soon as we got to know each other, we built a friendship straight away. We had a lot of fun playing with the kids. I felt good with them. We don't need to understand each other with words to become friends.

Bushmen language is very nice; it's a bit like music: more than using words they do 'clicks' with their tongues. I'm too shy to talk without knowing the language, except once. I said something to a woman by making sounds at random and also some 'clicks' with my tongue. She listened to me and she answered! I was worried: I don't even know what I said to her. I hope it wasn't a stupid thing.

Bushmen don't waste. When they have food they eat it until the last crumb. And their stomachs inflate, inflate! They respect nature too much to throw food away. For instance, they would never kill an animal that they don't really need.

They have no matches. They rub one stick on another really hard and then it makes fire. I've tried but it's not easy to do. You must learn for a long time.

They are magic too. For example, the witch doctor knows how to recognise the good place to avoid the bad spirits! And they talk to the moon. So every time it's full moon, Bushmen have a big celebration because to them the full moon is the Goddess.

We must admit that it's really beautiful to see the moon rise, very big, all round in the middle of the desert. During the celebration, men dance, but not the women. We clapped our hands. That's all. It's funny the way they dance. At the beginning, they dance normally then they become crazy.

Normally, the celebrations are secret; we have no right to film them or to photograph them. But because we were friends, they gave me a huge present of friendship by inviting me to stay with them.

Deep in my heart, I felt I was a Bushman. Just like them. On top of that I was dressed like one of them. But they are not the same colour as me. I'm white. And I will never be able to become the same colour as them.

Sometimes I want to quit speech.

I find it hard to understand why humans kill animals. It's stupid: if we kill them, there won't be any left and we won't be able to take pictures anymore. Pictures don't scare them, but guns do.

Dadou you're going on a trip
. . . I'd like you to come back
with . . . hmm . . . what could
you bring me? I know!
Come back quick!

Sometimes, we're forced to kill them, to protect ourselves or to eat. My mom told me that when I was a baby, she used to put a little revolver in the pushchair, in case a lion attacked us, because between the life of an animal and a human, it's generally always the human who is the most important. After all, I don't think Mom needed to shoot.

Bushmen, when they kill an animal to eat it, they always thank it for giving its life to feed the tribe. It's normal that they respect Nature.

It's not like hunters or poachers who don't care at all. It's horrible, but what can I do? And now I live in a flat in France and no longer there. And I'm a child. So the only thing I can do is to say that it's sad.

I like snakes. They are soft to touch. There are lots of people who are very, very scared of reptiles. To be scared is a horrible feeling, except when we're afraid because of a horror film, or when we've done something naughty, then it's funny; I love this. But real fears, we have to fight them otherwise we become crazy.

Me, as soon as I get a fright, or I feel impressed I try to fight it. For example, in swimming pools, there are *poutoums*. This is a robot that takes care of cleaning the bottom of the pool, and runs in the water and makes a noise. I call it the *poutoum* because it scares me so much that when it starts, my heart goes *'poutoum, poutoum'*. I dived under the water with Dadou several times to get near it and not be afraid anymore.

For snakes, it's the same. I like to help people to fight their fears. When they see me play with a snake, they think that if I can do it, they can too. So they touch it and they realize it's not so terrible. I even find this quite nice.

There's no such thing
as telling lies to my mom.
I used to tell some little lies,
but now I've stopped
because of trust.

These pictures are like those in a film. It's normal. Abu is an actor and maybe one day I will also be an actress. So we played the game together. He plays the role of the wild elephant charging. And me, I play the little girl from the bush who stops him by opening my arms. It worked out quite well: people who didn't know the story were quite impressed.

In reality, Abu would never think of hurting me. And one would be crazy to believe that a little girl can stop an angry wild elephant. And that her daddy would quietly sit there taking pictures. People are weird sometimes. They forget to think, and they imagine all kinds of things.

Everybody believes that a chameleon changes colour to hide, but this is not true. He changes colour according to his mood – if he is happy or angry, when he's afraid, if there's too much light, if it's night time, if it's cold . . .

I love, love, love this picture of my friend Leon, Leon the chameleon. Leon is so sweet. He has claws, which don't even hurt, and when he plays with my hair, it tickles! Well, of course sometimes it pinches . . .

I spend hours hunting grasshoppers for him. Just for the pleasure of seeing him squint and take his gummy tongue out.

It's really funny, and just like spitting out a big piece of chewing gum very fast. I used to look at him thinking, 'Go on Leon, go on'. With him the grasshoppers had no chance. But I don't care about grasshoppers. I just thank them to feed Leon. Animals eat one another, it's normal, and they were born for that. They were also born to feed humans, but just a little bit, not too much. That's life. For example, me, after Africa, I lived in Madagascar. There I raised lots of very, very sweet chicks, which ended up as big chickens. I love chicken, and it did not stop me from eating any.

But not the ones from my family. I only ate the dead chickens that we bought at the market, and that I didn't know personally.

One day, when we came back to Paris, we went to the butcher. There were lots of dead chickens that we could buy to eat, but I don't know why they still had their heads on. It made me feel so weird I thought I was going to faint. So I ran away.

I think that when we eat animals, it's better when they don't look like living animals.

My Dadou told me that a
chameleon's tongue goes
faster than a rocket.

When I'm not feeling comfortable somewhere, I'm ill at ease,
so strange things happen in my tummy. I call this the big
'gargouilli, gargouilla'. This is when my tummy goes up and
down. When it goes down, it goes away. But when it goes up, it
turns around again and again, cracking noises in my lungs.
When I was little, I used to think it hurt the bone of my heart.

It's so sad to leave a country that I would prefer it if we lived
nowhere at all. We would drive away with the truck, and camp
just like when we were in Namibia. But I don't think it's possible
anymore. I will do this when I'm a teenager, on holiday with
my boyfriend.

The uroplatus looks at you with
its weird eyes and jumps on you.
Its paws stick like suckers, and it
clinches everywhere!

Everybody has problems. I didn't have any during the time I lived in the bush in Africa. Then we came back to Paris. And we went to Madagascar. That's when it started.

We said to ourselves that Madagascar was lovely, but when we arrived we realized we were wrong.

There's a lot of nastiness there and children are really miserable. There are a lot who are ill and die.

A country can be magnificent, but if there is nastiness, it becomes catastrophic. I would rather forget about all this and only remember my chameleons from there: Madame Rose, Thelma, Louise, Mister Green and also big Max, the king of funny faces with his horrible temper.

Adventures: that's what I love in life.

Adults think that living with the wild animals of Africa is an adventure. They're completely mistaken. Adventures, for example, are going with your best friend to pinch some sweets and biscuits in the kitchen and to eat them on the sly in the toilet. Or inventing secret missions to fight your fears. Often, adults call these adventures foolishness.

That's because they don't know, or because they have forgotten . . .

If only life could always be lovely . . . It would not be boring if there were only incredibly exciting adventures.

We could even say that this is it, the secret of happiness: living adventures. But only if we choose adventures without problems.

I think problems arise when we grow up.

137

The Bip is my lemur from Madagascar. He was in love with my Barbie dolls, for real!

He used to stand up on his hind legs to kiss them on the mouth. I think that sometimes he thought he was Ken!

I left him there and I would rather not talk about him anymore to try to forget him. Thinking about it creates a big sadness in my heart.

In my schoolwork, I always want everything to be perfect. Before, it took me hours and hours and it was really tiring. But now I can write and learn a lot quicker. And when I've finished, I'm really happy with myself.

I love to learn a lot, but that depends on my teacher. During our travels, I study by correspondence with my mom or with a teacher. Sometimes I don't like to study with my mom very much. In Madagascar, my teacher's name was Perlette. She was my best friend amongst adults. She used to come to our house at 7:30 every morning, four days a week and for half a day on Wednesdays. Our school was on the terrace, in the shade. That was great too, because all the animals came to visit us: the guinea fowl who thought it was a helicopter, the chicks, the parrot who climbed on my head, the big rooster . . . We worked without realising it, because we turned the exercises into games.

At school, I talk too much because I have too many things to say. I'm a magpie; I have too many thoughts in my head.

I miss the future.

One night, something extraordinary happened to me. Incredible. Something that I had never seen before in my life: I saw a shooting star! I was busy talking to God – my hands were not gathered as in a prayer, I was just talking. I asked Him if I was the only little girl in the world who was living with animals, but that if there were others, I would not be jealous. I asked Him to welcome me when I come to Heaven. I also told Him that I loved Him a lot and that I thought of Him . . . And He sent me a shooting star!

I love to laugh. Lots and lots! And I also love to feel the wind in my hair, for example when we drive through the bush and I'm sitting on the roof, even if my neck gets cold. And I love meeting up with my best friend and cuddling. And I also like to see my boyfriend and hug him tightly in my arms. To have parents, a boyfriend and a best friend, that's all I need.

Tippi
My Book of
Africa

Struik Lifestyle
(an imprint of Random House Struik (Pty) Ltd)
Company Reg. No. 1966/003153/07
Wembley Square, Solan Road, Gardens 8001
PO Box 1144, Cape Town, 8000, South Africa

First published in South Africa by Struik Publishers in 2005
Reprinted in 2006, 2007 (twice), 2008
Reprinted by Struik Lifestyle in 2009, 2010, 2012, 2013

PUBLISHER: Linda de Villiers
MANAGING EDITOR: Cecilia Barfield
EDITOR: Irma van Wyk
DESIGNER: Helen Henn
PHOTOGRAPHERS: Sylvie Robert and Alain Degré
PROOFREADER: Helen de Villiers

ISBN 978-1-77007-029-5 (Print)
ISBN 978-1-43230-171-2 (ePub)
ISBN 978-1-43230-172-9 (PDF)

www.imagesofafrica.co.za

IMAGES OF AFRICA
PHOTO LIBRARY